Detective Stories

The First Case

Pete and Max in Action

MIT GEHEIMSCHRIFT FOLIE

Anni Mohn &
Martina Burghart-Vollhardt

circon

Baierbrunner Straße 27, 81379 München
Ausgabe 2022
5. Auflage

Text: Anni Mohn
Illustrationen: Martina Burghart-Vollhardt
Redaktion: Astrid Kaufmann
Übersetzung: Barbara Swayne
Fachredaktion: Stephanie Manz
Produktion: Ute Hausleiter
Titelabbildung: Martina Burghart-Vollhardt
Gestaltung: Roman Bold & Black, Köln
Umschlaggestaltung: Enrico Albisetti

ISBN 978-3-8174-2374-3
381742374/5

Besuchen Sie uns auf Instagram und Facebook: circonverlag

www.circonverlag.de

Pete's first case

Pete learns to read and to write. That is good! Now he can become a detective.

case	Fall
become	werden

Detectives have to write down many things. The names of suspects, for example.

have to	müssen
suspects	Verdächtige
often	oft
fun	Spaß
shouting	Geschrei

After school, Pete often goes
to the after-school club.
Normally it is fun there.
But today there is loud shouting.

‘My doll Wendy has been stolen!’,
Lily screams.
Ms Bell does not believe that.
Ms Bell is the teacher.

'I'm quite sure', Lily says. Everybody is looking for the doll. The children are checking all the bags.

doll	Puppe
(it) has been stolen	(es) wurde gestohlen
(to) scream	brüllen
(to) believe	glauben
quite sure	ganz sicher
(he/she) is looking for …	(er/sie) sucht nach …

But no Wendy!
'What does the doll look like?', Pete asks Lily.
'Why do you want to know that?', Lily asks him and crosses her arms.

Her friend Maya says to Pete: ‘She has brown hair and brown eyes. She wears a yellow dress. Her shoes are red, and her name is Wanda.’

Is that right?
What is the name of Lily’s doll?

(to) look like	aussehen
Why …?	Warum …?
(to) know	wissen
(to) cross	verschränken

'Nonsense', Lily says.
Her name is Wendy .
Pete takes a piece of paper and a pen. He sits down and draws.

nonsense	Blödsinn
(to) draw	zeichnen
almost	fast, beinahe
What is wrong …?	Was stimmt nicht …?

‘Does she look like this?’, he asks Lily.
He shows her the picture.
‘Almost’, Lily answers.

What is wrong with the picture?

‘These shoes are yellow. But Wendy wears red shoes’, Maya says.
‘Ah, well’, Pete says, a little upset.
‘That’s not important.’

‘That’s right’, Lily says. ‘Wendy is gone. I’m sure that my mum will buy me a new doll now.’

upset	verärgert
important	wichtig
(he/she) is gone	(er/sie) ist weg/ verschwunden
I’m sure …	Ich bin sicher …

The investigation begins

Pete goes home. He is thoughtful.
Who steals a doll?
Pete does not care much for dolls.

investigation	*hier:* Ermittlungen
thoughtful	nachdenklich
(to) steal	stehlen
not care much for dolls	sich nicht viel aus Puppen machen
Who else …?	Wer sonst …?

Then Pete has an idea.
It must be a girl!
Who else would steal dolls?

Pete stops and scratches his head.
There are many girls in the club.
Which one could it be?

Suddenly he remembers something. One girl knew everything about the doll! That is very suspicious.

Which girl knew everything about the doll?

(to) scratch	kratzen
Which one …?	Welches …?
suddenly	plötzlich
(to) remember	erinnern
(he/she) knew	(er/sie) wusste
suspicious	verdächtig

Maya !

Maya and her twin brother Max live nearby. Max and Pete are in the same year at school.

twin brother	Zwillingsbruder
nearby	in der Nähe
year	*hier:* Klasse
(he/she) is frightened	(er/sie) hat Angst
(he/she) hid	(er/sie) versteckte
naughty	frech

Pete is a little bit frightened of Max.
Once he hid Pete's shoes in school.
Very naughty!

The first suspect

Pete rings the doorbell of the house where Maya and Max live.
The mother opens the door.

doorbell	Türklingel
upstairs	oben
stairs	Treppe
(he/she) has discovered	(er/sie) hat entdeckt

'Maya and Max are upstairs', she says. Pete walks up the stairs. The door to Max's room is open. Pete stops.

What has Pete discovered?

On the bed lies a doll!
She wears a yellow dress
and red shoes.
Her hair is brown.

Is that Wendy? Pete runs to the bed.
'Hey!', Max shouts.

‘Did you steal Wendy?’,
Pete asks Max.
So, the thief was not a girl!
‘Who’s Wendy?’, Max asks.

Pete takes the doll.
Her eyes open.
No, it's not Wendy.

Why is it not Wendy?

thief	Dieb

The doll has [redacted].
Wendy has [redacted].
That's too bad.

That's too bad.	So was Blödes.
(to) tease	ärgern

‘Is that your doll?’, Pete asks.
‘Yes, that’s my doll’, Max says.
‘You want to tease me in school about that now?’

'No', Pete says. He is surprised.
'It's okay to have a doll!'
'What are you doing here?',
Max asks.
Pete tells him everything about
Wendy and the theft.

surprised	überrascht
theft	Diebstahl
more	*hier:* weitere
sometimes	manchmal
earlier	früher

Max is thinking: ‘It wasn’t Maya. You checked all the bags. But there are two more girls in your club and sometimes they go home earlier.’

That's right. Mary and Sophie always go to football training with Tim. They were not there when the children looked for Wendy.

They were not there …	Sie waren nicht da …
thrilled	begeistert
trail	Spur
(to) pull	ziehen

Pete is thrilled. A new trail!
Max pulls him towards the door.

A new trail

‘Perhaps the training isn’t over yet’, Max says.
The two detectives run to the football field.

The boys and girls are packing their bags.
'There!', Max shouts.

What has Max discovered?

In one of the backpacks there is a doll !
It’s Sophie’s backpack.

backpack Rucksack

Pete and Max go to Sophie
to stop her.
'You've stolen Wendy',
Pete says.

‘No, I haven’t!’, Sophie says. She is shocked. ‘I only took her with me!’

'So, you've stolen her', Pete says.
'No!', Sophie shouts. 'I found her
in the rubbish bin!'

(I) took her with me	(ich) nahm sie mit
(he/she) found	(er/sie) fand
rubbish bin	Mülleimer

Pete and Max look at each other.
They are surprised.
Wendy was in the rubbish bin?
‘She was under a lot of paper’,
Sophie explains.

'You must bring her back to Lily', Pete says. 'Perhaps somebody wanted to tease her.'

(to) explain	erklären
somebody	jemand

‘I think you’re right. Lily can be quite silly’, Max says. They go to Lily’s house and ring the doorbell.

quite	ziemlich
silly	blöd

Two super detectives

‘Here’s your doll’, Sophie says.
She gives Lily the doll.
‘I found her.’

'Great', Lily's mother says. 'Thank you!' But Lily is angry: 'Sophie! Why do you rummage through the rubbish?'

Pete stares at Lily with his mouth open. 'I think you have put her in the rubbish bin yourself!'

Why does Pete say that?

angry	ärgerlich
(to) rummage through …	herumkramen in …
(to) stare	anstarren
(you) have put	(du) hast gelegt
yourself	selbst

'How can Lily know about the rubbish bin?', Pete asks. He's proud. 'Sophie didn't talk about that.'

'Why did you do that?', Lily's mum asks.
She is angry.
'I just wanted a new doll', Lily says.
'And stolen is better than lost.'

proud	stolz
just	nur
lost	verloren

‘I would have given you a new doll for your birthday’, Lily’s mum says. ‘But you can forget about that now.’

'I don't care', Lily says.
'I've missed Wendy.'

(he/she) would have given	(er/sie) hätte gegeben
(to) forget	vergessen
I don't care.	Das ist mir egal.
I've missed…	Ich habe… vermisst

'You're a good detective', Max says to Pete on the way home.
'You are too', Pete says. 'Friends?'
'Friends', Max answers, and stretches out his hand.

too	auch
(to) stretch out	ausstrecken

Wörterverzeichnis

A

almost	fast, beinahe
angry	ärgerlich

B

backpack	Rucksack
become	werden
believe	glauben

C

case	Fall
(to) cross	verschränken

D

(he/she) has discovered	(er/sie) hat entdeckt
doll	Puppe
doorbell	Türklingel
(to) draw	zeichnen

E

earlier	früher
(to) explain	erklären

F

(to) forget	vergessen
(he/she) found	(er/sie) fand
(he/she) is frightened	(er/sie) hat Angst
fun	Spaß

G

(he/she) would have given	(er/sie) hätte gegeben
(he/she) is gone	(er/sie) ist weg/ verschwunden

H

have to	müssen
(he/she) hid	(er/sie) versteckte

I

I don't care.	Das ist mir egal.
important	wichtig
I'm sure …	Ich bin sicher …
investigation	*hier:* Ermittlungen

J

just	nur

K

(he/she) knew	(er/sie) wusste
(to) know	wissen

L

(to) look like	aussehen
(he/she) is looking for …	(er/sie) sucht nach …
lost	verloren

M

I've missed	ich habe vermisst
more	*hier:* weitere

N

naughty	frech
nearby	in der Nähe
nonsense	Blödsinn
not care much for dolls	sich nicht viel aus Puppen machen

O

often	oft

P

proud	stolz
(to) pull	ziehen
(you) have put	(du) hast gelegt

Q

quite	ziemlich
quite sure	ganz sicher

R

remember	erinnern
rubbish bin	Mülleimer
(to) rummage through …	herumkramen in …

S

(to) scratch	kratzen
(to) scream	brüllen
shouting	Geschrei
silly	blöd
somebody	jemand
sometimes	manchmal
stairs	Treppe
(to) stare	anstarren

(to) steal	stehlen
(it) has been stolen	(es) wurde gestohlen
(to) stretch out	ausstrecken
suddenly	plötzlich
surprised	überrascht
suspects	Verdächtige
suspicious	verdächtig

T

(to) tease	ärgern
That's too bad.	So was Blödes.
theft	Diebstahl
They were not there …	Sie waren nicht da …
thief	Dieb
thoughtful	nachdenklich
thrilled	begeistert
too	auch

(I) took her with me	(ich) nahm sie mit
trail	Spur
twin brother	Zwillingsbruder

U

upset	verärgert
upstairs	oben

W

What is wrong …?	Was stimmt nicht …?
Which one …?	Welches …?
Who else …?	Wer sonst …?
Why …?	Warum …?

Y

year	*hier:* Klasse
yourself	selbst